50 Ways to say "I Love you"

Beautiful quotes, notes, and sayings about love and what it does to us.

How do I love thee? Let me count the ways.
I love thee to the depth and breadth and height
My soul can reach, when feeling out of sight
For the ends of Being and ideal Grace.
I love thee to the level of every day's
Most quiet need, by sun and candle-light.
I love thee freely, as men strive for right;
I love thee purely, as they turn from praise,
I love thee with the passion put to use
In my old griefs, and with my childhood's faith.
I love thee with a love I seemed to lose
With my lost saints -I love thee with the breath,
Smiles, tears, of all my life! -and, if God choose,
I shall but love thee better after death.

- Elizabeth Barrett Browning

FORTUNE and LOVE favour the brave.

- OVID -

Mysterious love, uncertain treasure,
Hast thou more of pain or pleasure!
Endless torments dwell about thee:
Yet who would live, and live without thee!

~ Joseph Addison

The Fountains mingle with the Rivers
And the Rivers with the Oceans,
The winds of Heaven mix forever
With a sweet emotion;
Nothing in the world is single;
All things by a law divine
In one spirit meet and mingle.
Why not I with thine? --

See the mountains kiss high Heaven
And the waves clasp one another;
No sister-flower would be forgiven
If it disdained its brother,
And the sunlight clasps the earth
And the moonbeams kiss the sea:
What is all this sweet work worth
If thou kiss not me?

Pure LOVE
is as gentle as
the MOON
and as constant as
the SUN.

- James Lendall Basford

Love is the
GREATEST
refreshment
in LIFE.

~Pablo Picasso

to **LOVE DEEPLY**
IN ONE DIRECTION
MAKES US MORE LOVING
IN ALL OTHERS.

~Anne Sophie Swetchine~

The sweetest joy,
the wildest woe
is
LOVE.

Philip James Bailey

The hours I spend with you I look upon
as sort of a perfumed garden, a dim twilight,
and a fountain singing to it.
You and you alone make me feel that I am alive.
Other men it is said have seen angels,
but I have seen thee and thou art enough.

- George Edward Moore

A man is
only as good as
what he
LOVES.

~ Saul Bellow

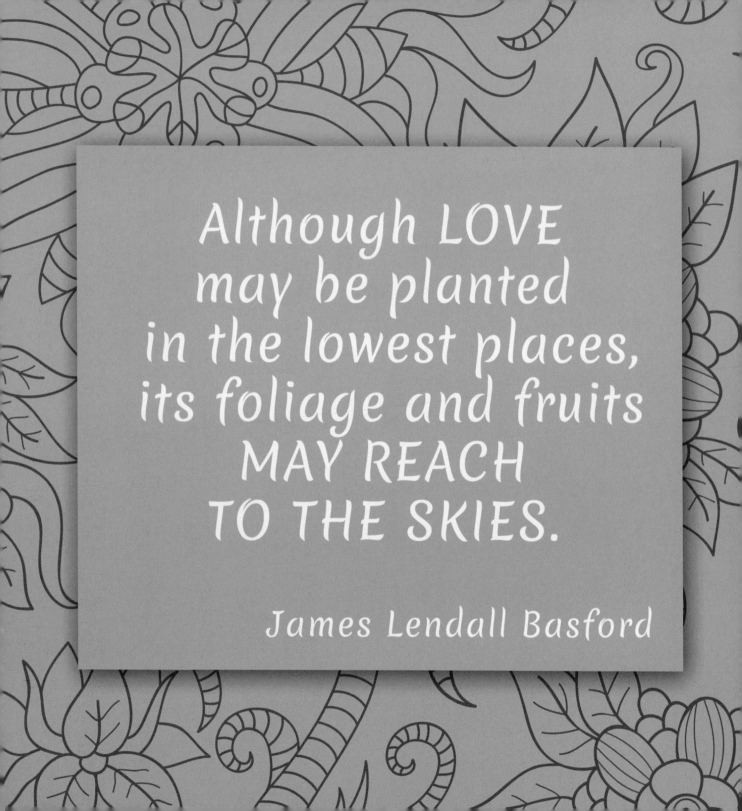

Although LOVE
may be planted
in the lowest places,
its foliage and fruits
MAY REACH
TO THE SKIES.

James Lendall Basford

Love is composed of a single soul inhabiting two bodies.

~Aristotle

Love is like a friendship
caught on fire.
In the beginning a flame,
very pretty, often hot and fierce,
but still only light and flickering.
As love grows older,
our hearts mature and
our love becomes as coals,
deep-burning and unquenchable.

- Bruce Lee

Dreaming of love, the ardent mind of youth
Conceives it one with passion's brief delights,
With keen desire and rapture.
But, in truth,
These are but milestones to sublime heights
After the highways, swept by strong emotions,
Where wild winds blow and blazing sun rays beat,
After the billows of tempestuous oceans,
Fair mountain summits wait the lover's feet.

The path is narrow, but the view is wide,
And beauteous the outlook towards the west
Happy are they who walk there side by side,
Leaving below the valleys of unrest,
And on the radiant altitudes above
Know the serene intensity of love.

Ella Wheeler Wilcox

Requited **love** is blissful state,
No mortals can themselves create:
We know not why to us 'tis given-
Enough: we know it is of Heaven.

James Lendall Basford

In peace, Love tunes the shepherd's reed;
In war, he mounts the warrior's steed;
In halls, in gay attire is seen;
In hamlets, dances on the green.
Love rules the court, the camp, the grove,
And men below and saints above;
For love is heaven, and heaven is love.

Sir Walter Scott

If you live to be a hundred,
I want to live to be
a hundred minus one day,
so I never have to live without you.

-A. A. Milne

Love is
a springtime plant
that perfumes everything
with its hope,
even the ruins to which it clings.

Gustave Flaubert

Love is like the wild rose-briar,
Friendship like the holly-tree,
The holly is dark when the rose-briar blooms
But which will bloom most contantly?
The wild-rose briar is sweet in the spring,
Its summer blossoms scent the air;
Yet wait till winter comes again
And who wil call the wild-briar fair?
Then scorn the silly rose-wreath now
And deck thee with the holly's sheen,
That when December blights thy brow
He may still leave thy garland green.

- Emily Bronte

Life

is the flower

for which love

is the honey.

~Victor Hugo~

How love came in I do not know,
Whether by the eye, or ear, or no;
Or whether with the soul it came
(At first) infused with the same;
Whether in part 'tis here or there,
Or, like the soul, whole everywhere,
This troubles me: but I as well
As any other this can tell:
That when from hence she does depart
The outlet then is from the heart.

Robert Herrick

*Falling in love consists
merely in uncorking
the imagination
and bottling
the common-sense.*

- Helen Rowland -

At the touch of LOVE
everyone becomes a POET.

Love is the part, and love is the whole;
Love is the robe, and love is the pall;
Ruler of heart and brain and soul,
Love is the lord and the slave of all!
I thank thee, Love, that thou lov'st me;
I thank thee more that I love thee.

Love is the rain, and love is the air,
Love is the earth that holdeth fast;
Love is the root that is buried there,
Love is the open flower at last!
I thank thee, Love all round about,
That the eyes of my love are lookingout.

Love is the sun, and love is the sea;
Love is the tide that comes and goes;
Flowing and flowing it comes to me;
Ebbing and ebbing to thee it flows!
Oh my sun, and my wind, and tide!
My sea, and my shore, and all beside!

Light, oh light that art by showing;
Wind, oh wind that liv'st by motion;
Thought, oh thought that art by knowing;
Will, that art born in self-devotion!
Love is you, though not all of you know it;
Ye are not love, yet ye always show it!

Faithful creator, heart-longed-for father,
Home ofour heart-infolded brother,
Home to thee all thy glories gather--
All are thy love, and there is no other!
O Love-at-rest, we loves that roam--
Home unto thee, we are coming home!

- George MacDonald

A goddess not inglorious in the skies
Is Venus, O sovereign, sea-born Venus.
Never with wild ungovern'd sway
Rush on my heart, and force it to obey:
For not the light'ning's fire,
Nor stars swift-darting through the sky,
Equal the shafts sent by this son of Jove,
When his hand gives them force to fly,
Kindling the flames of love.

Euripides

To be capable of steady friendship or lasting love, are the two greatest proofs, not only of goodness of heart, but of strength of mind.

William Hazlitt

*Love comforteth
like sunshine
after rain.*

William Shakespeare

When April bends above me
And finds me fast asleep,
Dust need not keep the secret
A live heart died to keep.

When April tells the thrushes,
The meadow-larks will know,
And pipe the three words lightly
To all the winds that blow.

Above his roof the swallows,
In notes like far-blown rain,
Will tell the little sparrow
Beside his window-pane.

O sparrow, little sparrow,
When I am fast asleep,
Then tell my love the secret
That I have died to keep.

- Sara Teasdale

Lovers don't finally
meet somewhere.
They're in each other
all along.

- Rumi -

If my lover were a comet
Hung in air,
I would braid my leaping body
In his hair.
Yea, if they buried him ten leagues
Beneath the loam,
My fingers they would learn to dig
And I'd plunge home!

Djuna Barnes

The
SUPREME HAPPINESS
of life is the conviction that
ONE IS LOVED;
loved for oneself,
or better yet,
loved despite oneself.

~Victor Hugo~

The moment
you have in your heart
this extraordinary
thing called love
and feel the depth,
the delight,
the ecstasy of it,
you will discover
that for you
the world
is transformed.

– Jiddu

The
HEART
has its reasons
that reason
knows
nothing of.

- Blaise Pascal -

The BEST and
MOST BEAUTIFUL
things in this world
cannot be seen or
even heard,
but MUST BE FELT
WITH THE HEART.
~ Helen Keller

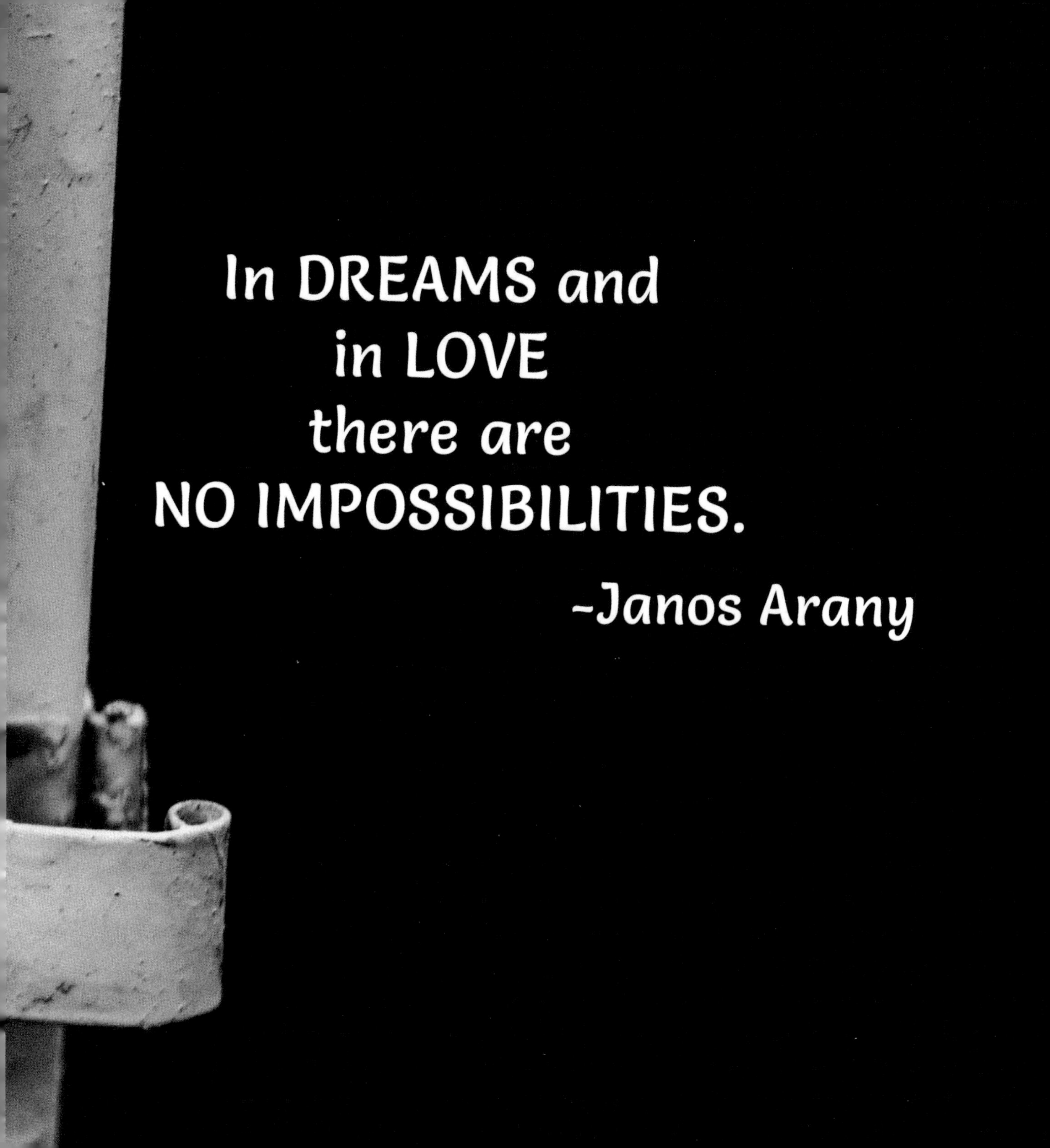

In DREAMS and
in LOVE
there are
NO IMPOSSIBILITIES.

-Janos Arany

LOVE
is a canvas
furnished by
Nature and
embroidered by
imagination.

~Voltaire

Love consists in this,
that two solitudes protect and touch
and greet each other.

- Rainer Maria Rilke

LOVE IS THE BEAUTY OF THE SOUL.

- Saint Augustine

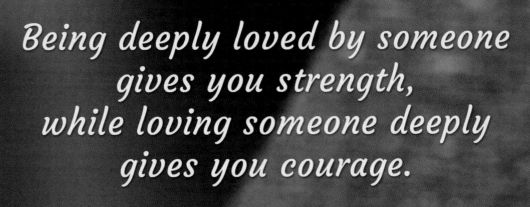

Being deeply loved by someone gives you strength, while loving someone deeply gives you courage.

- Lao Tzu

Where *there is* LOVE, *there is* LIFE.

– Mahatma Gandhi

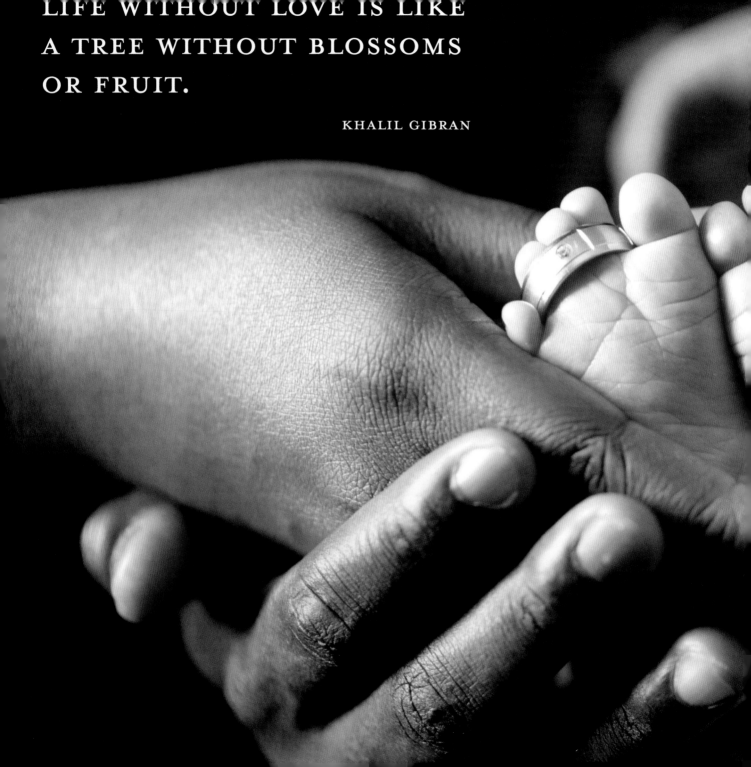

LIFE WITHOUT LOVE IS LIKE
A TREE WITHOUT BLOSSOMS
OR FRUIT.

KHALIL GIBRAN

And can you tell me Love is blind
Because your faults he will not find,
Because the image that he sees
Is one of splendid mysteries?
And if he lack the power to look
On what he will, as on a book,
And read therein the heart of it,
Why are his ways with wonder lit?
Why think you he should bind his eyes
And hide the many-tinted skies,
But that he sees too well to trust
The shadows on an orb of dust?
For he hath vision keener far
Than poring Thought's and Fancy's are
An inward vision, full and clear
When night has flung her mantle sheer
Across the world we stumble through
In search of Truth's evasive clue.
He looks, and straight there fall away
The flutt'ring rags of your array,
The far-fet gem, th' indecent drape,
The pads that mar the perfect shape,
And naked to his reverent view
Is beauty's self, essential you.

– John Le Gay Brereton –

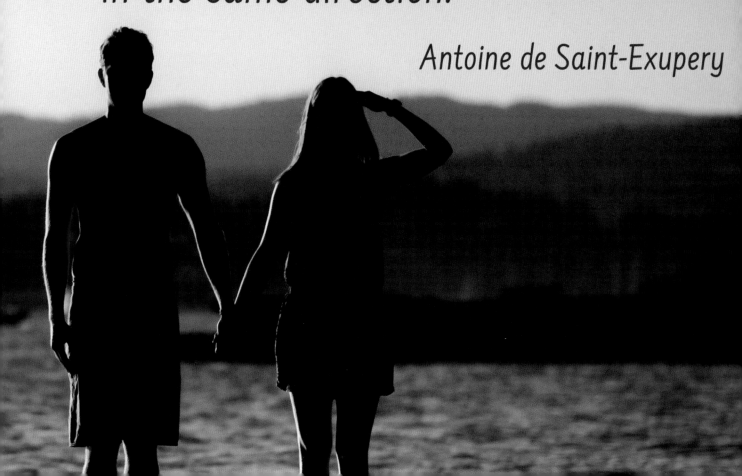

LIFE has taught us
that love does not consist
of gazing at each other,
but in LOOKING TOGETHER
in the same direction.

Antoine de Saint-Exupery

There is only
ONE HAPPINESS
in life,
TO LOVE and
BE LOVED

- George Sand

One word
frees us
from all of the
weight and pain of life.
That word
is LOVE.

-Sophocles

THERE IS NO
REMEDY FOR LOVE
BUT TO LOVE MORE.

- Henry David Thoreau

Come when the nights are bright with stars
    Or when the moon is mellow;
Come when the sun his golden bars
    Drops on the hay-field yellow.
Come in the twilight soft and gray,
Come in the night or come in the day,
Come, O love, whene'er you may,
    And you are welcome, welcome.

You are sweet, O Love, dear Love,
You are soft as the nesting dove.
Come to my heart and bring it rest
As the bird flies home to its welcome nest.

Come when my heart is full of grief
    Or when my heart is merry;
Come with the falling of the leaf
    Or with the redd'ning cherry.
Come when the year's first blossom blows,
Come when the summer gleams and glows,
Come with the winter's drifting snows,
    And you are welcome, welcome.

- Paul Laurence Dunbar

Love is patient, love is kind. It does not envy, it does not boast, it is not proud. It does not dishonor others, it is not self-seeking, it is not easily angered, it keeps no record of wrongs. Love does not delight in evil but rejoices with the truth. It always protects, always trusts, always hopes, always perseveres. Love never fails.

-St. Paul